BECOMING COMPATIBLE WORKBOOK

**Helping people get it right, get along, have fun
and achieve a successful working environment.**

MARK GUNGOR

BECOMING COMPATIBLE WORKBOOK
Published by Laugh Your Way America! LLC

©2017 by Laugh Your Way America! LLC
Mark Gungor, author

The FLAG PAGE, all graphics and screen shots are
the copyright of LIFE DISCOVERIES, INC.

FOUR STEPS TO DEFINING
YOUR PERSONAL MOTIVATIONS WORKSHEET

Your Name _____ Date _____

STEP 1: UNDERSTANDING YOUR COUNTRY

Home Country: _____   Control   Perfect

                                          Fun   Peace

A) I succeed by _____

B) and my country combination is: _____

STEP 2: UNDERSTANDING YOUR NATURE

Nature: Soft

                       Balancing

                       Hard

I succeed by: _____

STEP 3: UNDERSTANDING YOUR TOP FIVE MOTIVATORS - HOW YOU SUCCEED

A _____

B _____

C _____

D _____

E _____

STEP 4: UNDERSTANDING YOUR TOP TWO TALENTS

I am best at: _____

AND _____

Tear off at perforation

FLAG PAGE SOLUTIONS

CONTENTS

A FLAG PAGE STORY
MARK GUNGOR

When Mark Gungor conducted his first marriage seminar as an assistant pastor, he did so for one reason—nobody else in the church wanted to do it. The enthusiastic response he received from his first audience was just the tip of the iceberg. Today, he is one of the most sought-after international speakers on dating and marriage. Each year thousands of couples attend his Laugh Your Way to a Better Marriage® seminars. Mark's candid and comedic approach uses unforgettable illustrations and the power of laughter to teach proven principles that are guaranteed to strengthen any marriage.

"I love to inspire people's lives with truth and humor. There are a lot of performers that make people laugh, and there are a lot of speakers who give solid principles for living. I want to do both," Mark says. His take on marriage issues is refreshingly free of both churchy and psychological lingo. "Our secular culture over-romanticizes marriage and our Christian culture over-spiritualizes it. The reality is that relationships between men and women are very down to earth," Mark comments. "Laugh Your Way to a Better Marriage® is about helping couples get it right, get along, have fun, and achieve a successful marriage."

Mark is the Senior Pastor of Celebration Church—a multi-site church with three campuses across Wisconsin, and the CEO of Laugh Your Way America. He balances his pastoral duties with a rigorous travel schedule conducting marriage seminars, date nights, church services, as well as a speaker for civic and corporate events. Mark is one of the most requested speakers for the U.S. Army and his Laugh Your Way materials are used extensively by Chaplains and military personnel.

Mark has been featured on national broadcasts such as Focus on the Family, Life Today and ABC News. His videos on the differences between men and women are used in universities, colleges and schools. His best-selling books on relationships have been translated into multiple languages, impacting singles and couples world-wide.

"The key to helping people succeed in their working relationships is to focus on what's right about them...the Flag Page does just that."

Mark Gungor
Founder of Laugh Your Way America

It's more important to do what you love, than to do what you are good at...

FLAG PAGE SOLUTIONS

WHAT YOU NEED TO KNOW ABOUT THE FLAG PAGE®

Relationships can be complicated and yet hold so much potential for helping to create a fulfilling life. Fathers struggle to understand their daughters; mothers' relationships with their sons become strained, married couples misunderstand each other's needs, and boss/employee relationships can make it tough to go back to work the next day. Everyone wants to be validated and understood for who they are. When this happens, it brings out the best in people; when it doesn't, it brings out the worst.

Many people work hard to build and maintain their relationships but don't have the information to truly understand what makes other people tick. This session is designed to provide you with a guide to help you understand people—and YOURSELF! With Flag Pages in hand, you will be able to support, build up and believe in the people you care about.

In his book, ***Becoming Compatible***, Mark Gungor demonstrates the basics of The Flag Page® program. He also explains how the lack of knowledge about how people are motivated can lead to communication break down, creating problems and causing resentment.

This workbook makes it possible for you to go into more depth, fill out your personal motivations worksheet by better understanding your Flag Motivations and begin a plan to actually apply your Flag Page® to every day life.

WHAT THE FLAG PAGE IS AND IS NOT

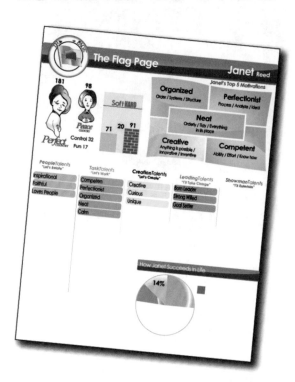

THE FLAG PAGE:

- Focuses on your strengths, passions and motivations.
- Is practical and simple.
- Helps define your purpose.
- Helps you to communicate and get along with those around you.
- Is fun and easy to use on a day-to-day basis.

THE FLAG PAGE IS NOT:

- A personality test.
- About your weaknesses.
- About what you can do or what you are good at.

The Flag Page® does a wonderful job of showing you what is great about you.

CONTROL COUNTRY

AT MY BEST	**AT MY WORST**
Born leader	Bossy
Tons of confidence	Impatient
Goal setter	Quick tempered
Independent	Demanding
Moves quick to action	Know it all
Bold	Arrogant

MY GREATEST NEED:

Give me **Appreciation** for what I **DO**.

- It's black and white, no gray.
- Shape of the country is a rectangle.
- Vehicle of this country is the bulldozer; make a way where there is no way.
- They need to lead and "get it done" as depicted by an orchestra conductor.
- When you use their own words such as "appreciate" and "accomplish" to communicate with them, they take interest in what you say.
- When supported, they live their greatest strengths, but when frustrated, show their greatest weaknesses.

FUN COUNTRY

AT MY BEST

Enthusiastic
Optimistic
Inspirational
Great sense of humor
Loves people
Sincere at heart

AT MY WORST

Talk too much
Exaggerates
Seems phony
Forgets responsibilities
No discipline
Easily distracted

- It's sunshine yellow for happiness.
- Shape of the country is a star.
- Vehicle of this country is the jet plane, for high speed and no limits.
- They love to socialize and have fun as depicted by a happy party.
- When you use their own words such as "really" and "great" to communicate with them, they take interest in what you say.
- When supported, they live their greatest strengths, but when frustrated, show their greatest weaknesses.

MY GREATEST NEED:

Give me Approval for how I ACT

PERFECT COUNTRY

AT MY BEST	AT MY WORST
Faithful	Remembers the negatives
Persistent	Moody, depressed
Idealistic	Feels guilty
Creative	Too much time planning
Organized	Standards too high
Thoughtful	Insecure around people

MY GREATEST NEED:

Give me **Sensitivity** to my **FEELINGS**.

- It's royal blue and pearl color.

- Shape of the country is a diamond.

- Vehicle of this country is the train, because the path must already be laid.

- They need the details to be right as depicted by a magnifying glass.

- When you use their own words such as "ideal" and "sensitive" to communicate with them, they take interest in what you say.

- When supported, they live their greatest strengths, but when frustrated, show their greatest weaknesses.

PEACE COUNTRY

AT MY BEST

Competent
Consistent
Witty
Patient
Peaceful
Good Listener

AT MY WORST

Fearful and worried
Can't make decisions
Too shy
Little self motivation
Resents being pushed
Resists change

- It's a calm lavender color.

- Shape of the country is a cloud.

- Vehicle of this country is the gondola, because there is no need for speed.

- They need to be efficient as depicted by laying in a hammock while mowing the lawn.

- When you use their own words such as "relax" and "easy way" to communicate with them, they take interest in what you say.

- When supported, they live their greatest strengths, but when frustrated, show their greatest weaknesses.

> MY
> GREATEST
> NEED:
>
> Give me
> **Respect**
> for who I
> **AM.**

STEP 1A:
UNDERSTANDING YOUR COUNTRY

Your **STEP 1** information will come from this page.
The example **Flag Page** below shows how to look at your own **Flag Page**
in order to choose the **Country** phase that applies to you.

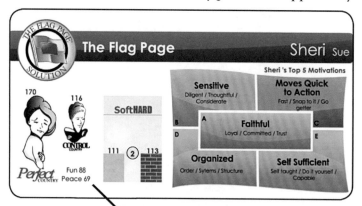

Country

Circle your Country definition from the choices below and
transfer to the Personal Motivations worksheet.

CONTROL COUNTRY

Controlling my environment by getting things done.

FUN COUNTRY

Creating warmer relationships by making it fun.

Perfect COUNTRY

Striving for the ideal by making things right.

Peace COUNTRY

Creating peaceful relationships by getting along.

FLAG PAGE® SOLUTIONS

STEP 1B:
UNDERSTANDING YOUR COUNTRY COMBINATION

Home and Adopted combinations describe
your value system in broad terms.

What is your combination? _____

Transfer your combination to the Personal Motivations Worksheet.

PERSONAL REFLECTION QUESTIONS

1. What was your initial reaction to your Flag Page? What surprised you? What confirmations were you given?

_____

_____

_____

2. How do you react when someone looks for what is wrong with you? Why does this fail to bring results?

_____

_____

_____

3. How do you react when someone seeks to understand what is right about you?

_____

_____

_____

4. Name two rewards that will come when you choose to support the values of the people you work with?

_____

_____

_____

5. Who do you know that comes to mind when you hear descriptions of the four countries?

_____

_____

_____

SOFT AND HARD NATURES

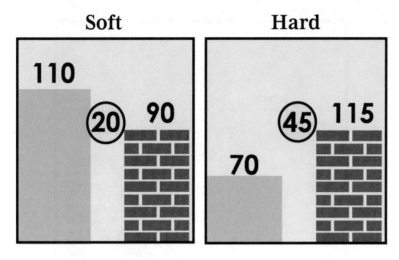

Soft Natured

Soft natured people are those with high Soft scores and low Hard scores. Soft natured people are more interested in people and relationships. Results are still in the car, but they take a back seat.

- Soft natured people are relational.
- Soft natured people are more flexible.
- Soft natured people see shades of gray.
- Soft natured people need lots of words.

Hard Natured

Hard natured people are those with high Hard scores and low Soft scores. Hard natured people tend to be more interested in accomplishing results. Relationships are still in the car, but they take a back seat.

- Hard natured people want results.
- Hard natured people are less flexible.
- Hard natured people see black and white.
- Hard natured people talk in bullet points.
-

**A gap number seen in the circle tells you if a person is Hard or Soft.
A gap of more than 15 to the Soft side equals a Soft natured person.
A gap of more than 15 to the Hard side is a Hard natured person.**

FLAG PAGE® SOLUTIONS

BALANCING PEOPLE

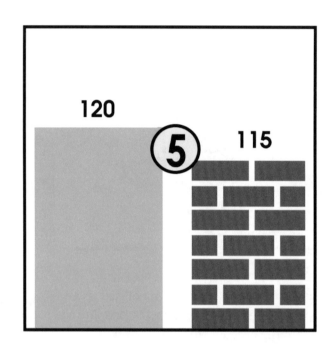

- Balancing people are those who vote highly for both Soft and Hard traits.

- A gap of 0 to 15 votes on the Soft/Hard scale indicates a Balancing person.

- Balancing people easily switch between the Soft nature and Hard nature.

- Balancing people find it easier to be both tough and fair.

- They relate well to both Soft and Hard natured people.

- Just as in the countries, the farther apart the votes, the more slowly the person moves towards the other nature.

- Soft natured people who are forced to be Hard can become very angry; they are out of their nature.

- Hard natured people who are forced to be Soft, can become very awkward.

- Remember that Balancing people are not "balanced" people who have arrived at a perfect place of balance. Instead, think of them as people who are constantly moving from Soft to Hard and back again.

STEP 2:
UNDERSTANDING YOUR NATURE

Your **STEP 2** information will come from this page.
The example **Flag Page** below shows how to look at your own **Flag Page**
in order to choose the **Nature** phase that applies to you.

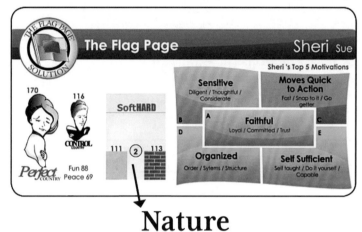

Nature

Circle your Country definition from the choices below
and transfer to the Personal Motivations worksheet.

Choose **SOFT** natured if your (gap)
number is 16 or higher on the Soft Side.

Creating better results through better relationships.

Choose **BALANCING** natured if your (gap)
number is between 0 and 15.

Accomplishing results by balancing
relationship issues with logic.

Choose **HARD** natured if your (gap)
number is 16 on the Hard side.

Achieving results in a logical way.

PERSONAL REFLECTION QUESTIONS

FLAG PAGE® SOLUTIONS

1. What characteristics of your own nature can you most relate to?

_____

_____

_____

2. What instances in life do you think Soft natured people are more favored?

_____

_____

_____

3. What instances in life do you think Hard natured people are more favored?

_____

_____

_____

4. How easy is it for you to relate to people who are not of the same nature as you?

_____

_____

_____

5. How can you facilitate better communication with this information?

_____

_____

_____

DEFINITION OF FLAG MOTIVATIONS

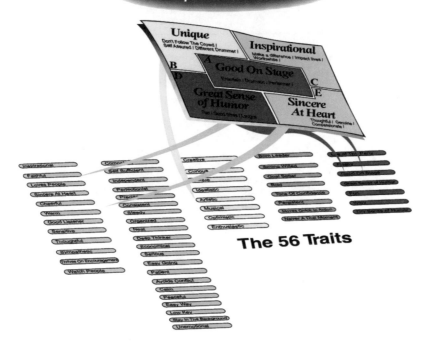

When people eliminate 51 other perfectly good traits to choose only five, these now become MAJOR MOTIVATIONS in their life.

- When a trait makes the top five list of the Flag, it is no longer just a trait, it is a motivation.

- Ultimately, all that matters is the definition a person gives their own motivation.

- Helping people express the meaning of these motivations starts with the support traits.

- Each of the 56 traits contain three support traits that help people explain their definition.

- By choosing one of the three support definitions under a motivation, a person can begin to define what their unspoken need is about.

The top five motivations explain how you succeed in life.

STEP 3: UNDERSTANDING YOUR TOP FIVE MOTIVATORS - HOW YOU SUCCEED

Your **STEP 3** information will come from this page.
The example shows where the **TOP FIVE Motivation**s are located in your **Flag Page.**
This is "Your Flag."

Let's look at your five Motivations:

Sample
Motivation: _____ *Faithful* _____

Definition: _____ *Trust* _____
(choose one of the support terms)

What it means to me: _____ *Please be dependable* _____
(See Appendix A for personal statements and transfer to worksheet)

For you to succeed, what would you need someone to do to support that?

_____ *If you say you are going to do something, please follow through.* _____
(transfer to worksheet)

A) **Motivation:** _____

Definition: _____
(choose one of the support terms)

What it means to me: _____
(See Appendix A for personal statements and transfer to worksheet)

For you to succeed, what would you need someone to do to support that?

_____
(transfer to worksheet)

B) **Motivation:** _____

    Definition: _____
                (choose one of the support terms)

What it means to me:_____
                    (See Appendix A for personal statements)

For you to succeed, what would you need someone to do to support that?

_____
                (transfer to worksheet)

C) **Motivation:** _____

    Definition: _____
                (choose one of the support terms)

What it means to me: _____
                    (See Appendix A for personal statements)

For you to succeed, what would you need someone to do to support that?

_____
                (transfer to worksheet)

D) **Motivation:** _____

    Definition: _____
                (choose one of the support terms)

What it means to me: _____
                    (See Appendix A for personal statements)

For you to succeed, what would you need someone to do to support that?

_____
                (transfer to worksheet)

E) **Motivation:** _____

    Definition: _____
                (choose one of the support terms)

What it means to me: _____
                    (See Appendix A for personal statements)

For you to succeed, what would you need someone to do to support that?

_____
                (transfer to worksheet)

THE FIVE TALENT FAMILIES

Five Talent Families

Look at your top two Talent Families. These lists will help you understand what the two Talent Families are about. These expanded talent stories give you a concise description of each Talent Family.

Most people find them to be accurate descriptions that match up with how they think of themselves. These top two Talent Families are where you will find the most fulfillment and usually the most skill.

People Talents
"Let's Relate"

- Caring for less fortunate
- Being genuine and real
- Compassion for the hurting
- Feeling what people feel
- Understanding points of view
- Enjoy communication
- Looking for ways to help
- Thinking of needs to fill

Creation Talents
"Let's Create"

- Creating new ideas
- Seeing old things in new ways
- Thinking of potential
- Discussing possibilities
- Exploring options
- Searching out choices
- Making plans
- Building new innovations

Showman Talents
"I'll Entertain"

- Presenting ideas
- Entertaining others
- Acting funny
- Making people laugh
- Keeping things light
- Finding humor in anything
- Enjoying the clever
- Forgetting the past
- Laughter is the best medicine

Task Talents
"Let's Work"

- Do the work yourself
- Hands on
- Skills
- Accomplishments
- Staying busy
- Being active
- Staying involved
- Using talents, abilities

Leading Talents
"I'll Take Charge"

- Taking charge
- Being up front
- Being responsible
- Giving direction
- Giving others vision
- Making hard decisions
- Being disciplined
- Living an example
- Setting expectations

STEP 4: UNDERSTANDING YOUR TWO TOP TALENT FAMILIES

Your **STEP 4** information will come from this page. Find your **TOP two Talent Families** by looking for the largest sections of the pie graph on your **Flag Page**.

These are your **TOP two Talent Families**. Below look for the two icons that represent your two strongest Talent Families and copy that phrase into Step 4 of your worksheet.

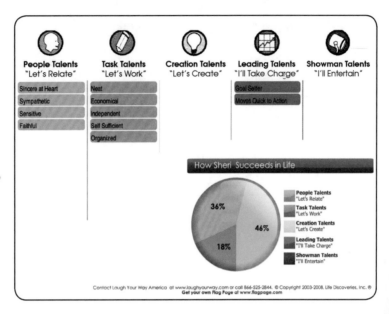

People Talents "Let's Relate"	Task Talents "Let's Work"	Creation Talents "Let's Create"	Leading Talents "I'll Take Charge"	Showman Talents "I'll Entertain"
Sincere at Heart	Neat		Goal Setter	
Sympathetic	Economical		Moves Quick to Action	
Sensitive	Independent			
Faithful	Self Sufficient			
	Organized			

How Sheri Succeeds in Life

- 36%
- 46%
- 18%

- **People Talents** "Let's Relate"
- **Task Talents** "Let's Work"
- **Creation Talents** "Let's Create"
- **Leading Talents** "I'll Take Charge"
- **Showman Talents** "I'll Entertain"

Contact Laugh Your Way America at www.laughyourway.com or call 866-525-2844. © Copyright 2003-2008. Life Discoveries, Inc. ®
Get your own Flag Page at www.flagpage.com

Connecting and relating with people to create more unity AND working on projects that fulfill me.

Working on projects that fulfill me AND doing it for the benefit of myself and others.

Connecting and relating to people AND solving problems with new solutions that benefit everyone.

Creating new solutions that solve problems AND bringing people better lives.

Connecting and relating to people AND leading them to their potential to accomplish more.

Leading people toward their potential to accomplish more AND improving the lives of everyone I lead.

Connecting and relating to people AND finding more ways to lighten their lives through my humor.

Sharing my light and lively humor AND helping people to become a little happier.

Working on projects that fulfill me AND creating ideas that solve problems with new solutions.

Solving problems, creating innovative solutions AND getting involved in projects that fulfill me most.

Working on projects that fulfill me AND being the one who takes charge of those projects.

Leading people to their potential to accomplish more AND working with projects that fulfill me.

Working on projects that are fun for me AND allowing people to enjoy themselves around my humor.

Finding more ways to lighten the load for people AND working with projects I find fulfilling and fun.

Solving problems that make things better AND leading people in the application of my new ideas.

Leading people to their potential of accomplishing more AND creating innovative improvements.

Solving problems by creating new solutions AND creating fun and enjoyment for people.

Finding ways to lighten the load of others AND using my creativity to develop fun ideas for people.

PERSONAL REFLECTION QUESTIONS

FLAG PAGE® SOLUTIONS

1. How do you feel when you look at your Flag Page motivations?

_____

_____

_____

2. How do you feel when you look at someone else's Flag Page motivations?

_____

_____

_____

3. What could stand in the way of supporting each other's motivations on an everyday basis?

_____

_____

_____

4. What do you now understand about yourself that you didn't before doing the Flag Page?

_____

_____

_____

FLAG PAGE SUMMARY

The Flag Page is a very simple way to understand a very complex subject...PEOPLE! In everyday life, we don't need a complete analysis of our husband or wife, co-worker, or friend. What we need is a kind of shorthand that gets us right to the point. How should I treat this person? What should I expect from this person? How can I support who this person really is? Use the Flag Page to answer the questions that matter most.

SUPPORT THESE AND COOPERATION IS MORE THAN POSSIBLE!

The four Countries explain why we act the way we act.

The natures explain why we react the way we react.

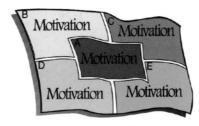

The Flag shows what our five greatest motivations are.

*Creation*Talents "Let's Create"   *Leading*Talents "I'll Take Charge"

*Showman*Talents "I'll Entertain"

*People*Talents "Let's Relate"   *Task*Talents "Let's Work"

The Talent Families help us focus on where we succeed most in life.

UNDERSTANDING THE WHY

Read the following experience from Steven Covey, best-selling author of *The Seven Habits of Highly Effective People*. It conveys the importance of understanding the WHY of situations. When you understand the WHY, it changes your perspective.

Covey was on a New York subway train on Sunday morning. People were sitting quietly, some reading newspapers, some dozing, others simply contemplating with their eyes closed.

Then, at one stop, a man got on with his children. The children were yelling, throwing things, even grabbing people's newspapers. Naturally, the passengers were upset, but the father just sat there, doing nothing. Covey just couldn't believe that this man could be so insensitive as to let his children run wild and not do anything about it.

So finally, with what he thought was admirable restraint and patience, Covey said to the man, "Sir, your children are really disturbing a lot of people. I wonder if you couldn't control them a little bit more?"

The man lifted his gaze as if coming into consciousness for the first time and said, "Oh, you're right. I guess I should do something about it. We just came from the hospital where their mother died about an hour ago. I don't know what to think, and I guess they don't know how to handle it either."

Covey says, "Can you imagine what I felt at that moment? Suddenly I saw things differently. Because I saw differently, I felt differently, I behaved differently. My irritation vanished. I didn't have to worry about controlling my attitude or my behavior. My heart was filled with this man's pain. Feelings of compassion and sympathy flowed freely. "Your wife just died? Oh, I'm so sorry! Can you tell me about it? What can I do to help?"

Nothing changed in that subway car. All was the same: The same people, the same irritation, the same kids. What did change was a way of seeing it all.

Notes:

_____

_____

_____

_____

_____

_____

_____

_____

_____

_____

_____

_____

_____

_____

_____

_____

_____

_____

_____

_____

_____

_____

Notes:

FLAG PAGE® SOLUTIONS

Notes:

_____

_____

_____

_____

_____

_____

_____

_____

_____

_____

_____

_____

_____

_____

_____

_____

_____

_____

_____

_____

FLAG PAGE® SOLUTIONS

WHAT HAPPENS WHEN PEOPLE ARE STRESSED?

1.

a. They become _____

b. They become less _____

c. They either become more _____ or_____

2. What do you think will happen for:

a. Control Country _____

b. Fun Country _____

c. Perfect Country _____

d. Peace County _____

3. Strategies for dealing with different countries under stress:

a. Control Country

Let them finish _____

Problem Solve with _____

b. Fun Country

Stay out of their way until they are _____

Problem Solve with _____

c. Perfect Country

Draw them out with _____

Problem Solve with _____

d. Peace Country

Draw them out with _____

Problem solve with _____

HOW DOES THE FLAG PAGE INFORMATION HELP WITH OTHER PEOPLE WHEN THEIR FLAG PAGE IS NOT AVAILABLE?

Listening and observing are your best tools:

1. Words they use and how they use them:

_____

_____

2. What is the message you hear by what they say or what they do?

_____

_____

_____

3. What they say and how they act shows what is important to them.

    a. People show what is important to them by spending_____and_____on it.

    b. People show what is important to them by spending_____on it.

4. Now that you have a general idea of what country they are from:

    a. Start using their language and style when talking to them.

    b. Focus on the goal from their point of view.

    c. Find common ground to work from.

    d. Walk along side them to solve a problem.

Answers are on page 34

FLAG PAGE® SOLUTIONS

Answers:

Page 32

1.
    a. More like their home country in that they operate more exclusively within their home country
    b. versatile
    c. Aggressive (fight), passive (flight)

2.
    They will show more fight or flight tendencies. Also, look at the words located under each country's "At my worst"

    a. Control Country: aggressive (fight) – Bossy, Impatient, Quick Tempered, Demanding, Know it all, Arrogant
    b. Fun Country: aggressive (fight) – Talk too much, Exaggerates, Seems Phony, Forgets Responsibilities, No Discipline, Easily Distracted
    c. Perfect Country: passive (flight) – Remembers the negatives, Moody, Depressed, Feel guilty, Too much time planning, Standards too high, Insecure around people
    d. Peace: passive (flight) – Fearful & worried, Can't make decisions, Too shy, Little self-motivation, Resents being pushed, Resists change

3.
    a. Control Country: Talking, task options
    b. Fun Country: finished talking, fun as a result of resolution (Once this is over, we can get back to fun)
    c. Perfect Country: problem solving questions, recommendations as opposed to options
    d. Peace Country: feeling questions, showing how it will result in everyone getting along

Page 33

1.
    Look for country words they use, i.e. "get it done", "Accomplish", "Good Time", "Happy", "Ideal", "Right", "No Hassle", "The easy way"

2.
    Listen for phrases they use, like:
    Control Country – Get it done
    Fun Country – Have Fun
    Perfect Country – Get it Right
    Peace Country – Get along

3.
    a. Time, effort
    b. money

APPENDIX A

56 FLAG PAGE TRAITS and Support Terms/Personal Statements

Artistic – Doing more to make an attractive environment
- Good Taste: I appreciate the finer things / I know what is appropriate / Be classy
- Stylish: I know when it's good taste / When it looks right, I know it / Appearance does matter
- Skilled: I'm competent at this / There's a right way and a wrong way / I know what I'm doing

Avoids Conflict – Staying out of tension and trouble
- Safe: Let's keep things calm / Everyone's feelings matter / I do better without pressure
- Secure: I need to trust you / Can you reassure me? / I need your commitment
- Getting Along: Let's live the golden rule / We can work it out / Let's accept our differences

Bold – Doing what's daring
- Determined: I'll make this happen / Persistence always wins / Roadblocks are no problem
- Tough: If you can't stand the heat, get out of the kitchen / You've got to be strong / I can endure
- Takes A Stand: Together let's make it better / Let's do the right thing / Don't compromise the standard

Born Leader – Taking charge and moving ahead
- Responsible: We have promises to keep / Do what you said you would do / I'll handle it
- Empowering: I'll back you all the way / I know you can do this / I can contribute
- Takes Charge: Here's how this needs to go / I've got a plan / Work together and get it done

Calm – Creating the most stress-free life
- Quiet: Let's keep our wits about us / Calm down and relax / Let's take a moment and think
- Anchored: You can depend on me / I'll always be there / I don't waiver on what's right
- Levelheaded: Let's keep an even keel / Take it easy / Stay calm, it's ok now

Cheerful – Being pleasant under any circumstance
- Happy: I like who I am / That's the way it ought to be / Let's all just get along
- Pleasant: Let's all just enjoy ourselves / Just enjoy the ride / We can all play nice
- Friendly: Let's get together / Let's accept each other / We have things in common

Competent – Being good at anything you begin
- Ability: I can do this / I can do it, no problem / There's always a way
- Effort: Let's give it some elbow grease / I need to give it all I've got / Let's go the extra mile
- Know-how: I know how to do this / I see a way to do it / I must get it done efficiently

Consistent – Making things stable and steady
- Stable: Let's keep this the same / If it's not broke, don't fix it / Leave well enough alone
- Even: We need to keep it going / Keep it the way it was / I need it to be predictable
- Predictable: It needs to stay like this / It's like this for a reason / Leave well enough alone

Creative – Finding new ways to solve problems
- Anything is possible: There's another way / There's an opportunity here / There are no limits to what I can do
- Innovative: I've got a better way / Look at it my way / Let's try a new approach
- Inventive: Let's make a way to do it / I can find another way / It's in here somewhere

FLAG PAGE® SOLUTIONS

Curious – Keep exploring, asking and searching
- Search: I need to look into this more / There's gotta be more to it / I want to know the answer
- Explore: I gotta get out of here / I need to investigate this more / I'm looking for possibilities
- Answers: Let's find a way / How does this REALLY work? / Tell me what you really mean

Deep Thinker – Analyze everything in order to understand it
- Analyze: I need to understand that / What's the real meaning here? / There's more to it than this
- Thoughtful: I'm thinking of you / Here's something else to consider / I need to know why
- Introspective: I'm going to find a way / Let me think about this / Look inward to solve problems

Dry Sense of Humor – Coming up with unexpected humor
- Witty: There's a clever way to say that / I see it as rather amusing / I like the unexpected
- Unconventional: There's another way / Watch the crowd and go the other way / I take the unique approach
- Comic: Let's look at the lighter side / Life's too short not to laugh / I see the humor in it

Easy Going – Allowing people to be themselves
- Calm: You should chill out / Let's just accept each other / I'm relaxed and aware
- Go with the flow: Let's take it easy / Let's go with it / Whatever.... / There's always tomorrow
- Laid back: Just chill out / Go with the flow / No reason to get upset yet

The Easy Way – Taking the path of least resistance
- Efficient: Let's not waste our energy / There's a better way to get there / Plan it, then do it
- Low key: Let's just stay calm / There's no reason to get upset / Don't rock the boat
- At your own pace: I'll get back to you on that / Let's just take it easy / I'm done when I'm done

Economical – Finding more ways to be financially secure
- Save money: I can get it for less / Now that's a deal / I'll get just what I really want
- Careful: Let's be cautious about this / Make sure it's justified / Plan for everything
- Thrifty: Let's do the most efficient thing / Here's another way to save / I need to get the best value

Enthusiastic – Showing people how I feel
- Upbeat: Let's make this positive / I like never a dull moment / Let's take the high road
- Energy: I make things happen / There's a lot more we can do / Let's pick up the pace!
- Happy: I like who I am / That's the way it ought to be / Let's all just get along

Faithful – Being loyal and true to a chosen few
- Loyal: I'm here for you no matter what / You can trust me / Be true to yourself
- Committed: I'm no quitter / I'm secure with your commitment / I'm dedicated to the cause
- Trust: I'll be there for you / Be there for me and I'll be there for you / Please be dependable

Flashy – Standing out when going out
- Glamour: I need to be a class act / Everything needs the right look / Fashion really does matter
- Stand out: Hey! Watch this! / You'll get a kick out of this / Here's something you'll really like
- Show stopper: I think you're going to enjoy this / Hey! Watch me now! / I'll knock your socks off

Fun – Looking for good times with everyone
- Laughs: Let's all lighten up / Let's forget our troubles / Let's just have a good time
- Enjoy: I gotta love it / Enjoy every moment / Let's experience it together
- Light hearted: It's best if we all lighten up / Why not forget our troubles / Take it easy

Goal Setter – Staying focused on what I really want
- Achiever: Let's do that now / I can do more than this / Let's take it to the next level
- Accomplish: I made this! / I'll handle it from here / I love being a winner
- Driven: I'm determined to get this done / I need to get a result / Let's do something valuable

Good Listener – Being willing to hear everyone's ideas
- Patient: I can be flexible / I can accept you as you are / Let me learn about you so I can help
- Attentive: I'm all ears / I noticed that / I'm paying attention
- Courteous: I want to consider your feelings / Let me know how you're feeling / I think of you first

Good on Stage – Reaching the crowd by being up front
- Entertain: Let me have your attention / You're gonna love this! / I love making music
- Dramatic: I'll leave you spellbound / I can make it spectacular / This is going to move you
- Performer: Ok, now watch this / You're going to love this / I want to teach you something

Great Sense of Humor – Keeping my knack for creating laughs
- Fun: Let's forget our troubles / I love it when you accept me / We can connect
- Good times: Let your hair down for a change / Don't take yourself too seriously / Let's cut loose
- Laughs: Let's all lighten up / Let's forget our troubles / Let's just have a good time

Idealistic – Knowing it can always be better than this
- Right: That's the way it ought to be / I know when it's right / It's either right or it's wrong
- Perfect: We can make it exactly right / It can be better than this / Here's where we can improve it
- Standards: There's a right and wrong way / I won't compromise my values / Let's improve our ways

Independent – Standing on my own two feet
- Self-sufficient: I'll take care of this / I'll rely on me / I'm very capable
- Competent: Do it right the first time / Just do your very best / Show you care about your work
- In control: It's gotta go this way / I know what's going on / I've got the plan

Inspirational – Finding ways to make a real difference
- Make a difference: There's much more we can do / Here's where we can make an impact / I see the need
- Impact lives: We're going to make it better / I'm gonna shake your tree / I'm thrilled to see you do better
- Worthwhile: Let's focus on what matters / I need work to mean something / Let's do something valuable

Life of the Party – Making it happen so everybody has fun
- Exciting: Wait till you see this! / Let's have fun and connect / It's intensely fun
- Happy-go-lucky: Let's forget our troubles and have fun / Relax and enjoy the ride / Nothing bothers me
- Center of attention: Hey! Watch this! / You'll get a kick out of this / Here's something you'll really like

Loves People – Making sure everyone knows they are ac
- Acceptance: I'm flexible / Let's be supportive / I'm grateful for what we've got
- Warm: Let's get connected / Let's find what's in common / Let's relate
- Caring: Are you OK? / I want to know how you're doing / What can I do to help?

Low Key – Keeping a low profile to not disturb anyone
- Stable: Let's keep this the same / If it's not broke, don't fix it / Leave well enough alone
- Secure: I need to trust you / Can you reassure me? / I need your commitment
- Calm: You should chill out / Let's just accept each other / I'm relaxed and aware

Moves Quick To Action – Doing it now rather than waiting too long
- Fast: Why not do it now? / Let's get to the point / Is it done yet?
- Snap to it: Let's make it happen / No time like the present / Let's get 'er done!
- Go-getter: This is going to be good / Let's get started now / Ambition is good

Musical – Expressing my deepest feeling through music
- Rhythm: I like a steady routine / And the beat goes on / Let's be consistent
- Entertain: Let me have your attention / You're gonna love this! / I love making music
- Meaning: There's gotta be more / I've got to make a difference / I will impact your life

Neat – Putting everything in its place
- Orderly: Let's keep everything working / Things are as they should be / Keep it all in place
- Tidy: We can clean this up / Let's straighten some things out / We need an orderly environment
- Everything in its place: Let's make it productive / It's better when it's neater / Order makes things right

Never A Dull Moment – Keeping a fast pace so it's never dull
- Hop to it: I'll get right on that / Why not do it now? / No time like the present
- Fast-paced: Let's make something happen now / You'll need to keep up / Get it moving
- Busy: I'll get right on that / There is always something to do / The more we plan, the more we'll do

Optimistic – Believing that most everything is possible
- Anything is possible: There's another way / There's an opportunity here / There's no limit to what I can do
- Cooperative: Let's work together on this / We should join forces / Let's work as a team
- Potential: There's more we can do / It can always be better than this / I have a vision for it

Organized – Bringing structure and order to chaos
- Order: All is as it should be / With order we'll get things done / Don't mess up my world
- Systems: Let's go at this step by step / I know exactly where it is / Be more productive
- Structure: Let's stay the course / Let's do this right/ We need a system

Patient – Allowing people to be who they are around me
- Accepting: I can go along with that / Just live and let live / It is what it is
- Thoughtful: I'm thinking of you / Here's something else to consider / I need to know why
- Understanding: I know how you feel / I see the potential / I'm sympathetic to your problem

Peaceful – Giving people more ways to get along
- Calm: You should chill out / Let's just accept each other / I'm relaxed and aware
- Relaxed: We should just take it easy / Just chill out / THIS is what it's all about
- Adaptable: You need to roll with the punches / Let's work with what we've got / I can go with it

Perfectionist – Making it exactly right
- Process: Let's take it step-by-step / Follow the system / We should analyze this first
- Analyze: I need to understand that / What's the real meaning here? / There's more to it than this
- Ideal: There must be a better way / I think we should do more / Here's something you haven't considered

Persistent – Never giving up no matter the obstacles
- Disciplined: I know what I've got to do / Nothing takes me off my goal / Where there's a will there's a way
- Driven: I'm determined to get this done / I need to get a result / Let's do something valuable
- Committed: I'm no quitter / I'm secure with your commitment / I'm dedicated to the cause

FLAG PAGE® SOLUTIONS

Precise – Paying attention to the important details
- Exact: Here's something I've noticed / Take a look at this / I must have all the facts
- Details: It's the little things that count / It's all in the details / Pay attention
- Accurate: I can back that up / I know this is true / I know how to relate and respond

Self Sufficient – Doing it my own way on my own terms
- Self-taught: Look what I found / Here's what I know now / I learn it then do it
- Do-it-yourself: I'll handle this / Easier to do it than to explain it / If I want it done right, I'll do it
- Capable: I can do this / I've got a good handle on it / I'll take it from here

Sensitive – Feeling what everyone feels
- Diligent: I just won't give up / Stick with the plan / We need to stay steady now
- Thoughtful: I'm thinking of you / Here's something else to consider / I need to know why
- Considerate: How do you feel? / How can I help? / All sides should be considered

Sincere At Heart – Making sure that I and others are genuine and fair
- Thoughtful: I'm thinking of you / Here's something else to consider / I need to know why
- Genuine: It's gotta be real / Just be yourself / I accept who you are
- Compassionate: I make life easier / I accept you as you are / I know where you're coming from

Serious – Understanding what really does matter
- Standards: There's a right and wrong way / I won't compromise my values / Let's improve our ways
- Focused: Keep your eye on the ball / I will not be distracted / We must stay on task
- Important: I think this could be significant / Let's focus on what matters / We need a purpose

Stay in the Background – Making sure that all is well and safe
- Supportive: Is there something I can do? / Where can I help? / Just tell me what you need
- Encouraging: Let me help you with that / I see your potential / I really believe in you
- Give credit to others: I admire what you've done / I can see your talent / You've got a knack for this

Steady – Being the one who is solid as a rock
- Predictable: It needs to stay like this / It's like this for a reason / Leave well enough alone
- Productive: There's something else we should do / Let's keep it moving / We'll get it done
- Stable: Let's keep this the same / If it's not broke, don't fix it / Leave well enough alone

Strong willed – Making sure my opinions are known and respected
- Determined: I'll make this happen / Persistence always wins / Roadblocks are no problem
- Leadership: I see your true potential / There's more to you than you think / Are you with me or not?
- Focused: Keep your eye on the ball / I will not be distracted / We must stay on task

Sympathetic – Showing people how much I understand
- Responsive: Let me know what you need / Share so we can all learn / I can take care of that
- Agreeable: I can see your point of view / I know how you feel / I'll do what you like most
- Understanding: I know how you feel / I see the potential / I'm sympathetic to your problem

Thoughtful – Thinking about the needs of other people
- Considerate: How do you feel? / How can I help? / All sides should be considered
- Caring: Are you OK? / I want to know how you're doing / What can I do to help?
- Warm: Let's get connected / Let's find what's in common / Let's relate

FLAG PAGE® SOLUTIONS

Thrives on Encouragement – Finding people who will believe in me
- Nurture: How did I do? / I thrive with your support / Let me help you with that
- Build up : Keep good feedback coming / I love it that you noticed / Thanks for being in my corner
- Believe: Tell me what's good about me / Consider my good points / Make me a priority

Tons of Confidence – Showing that I am certain and why I am
- Self-assured: I know I can do this / I'll handle this now / I know who I am
- Certain: I know what I'm talking about / I'm sure of this / This is going to work out
- Leader: There's more to you than this / I see your true potential / I know you can

Unemotional – Being the one who is unshaken and steady
- Unshaken: I'd rather not react/ Maybe, Maybe not / That remains to be seen
- Steady: Let's keep it the way it is / We'll just see / Don't wreck my routine

Unique – Seeing and doing things like no one else ever will
- Don't follow the crowd: They just don't understand / I'm happy I'm different / I've got the better idea
- Self-assured: I know I can do this / I'll handle this now / I know who I am
- Different drummer: I see it differently / Let's try it a different way / The crowd doesn't get it

Warm – Finding ways to understand and connect with more people
- Approachable: I'm always open to ideas / Talk with me, I'm safe / I see your point of view
- Genuine: It's gotta be real / Just be yourself / I accept who you are
- Real: I need a connection / Just be honest with me / Please be genuine

Watch People – Always staying the keen observer of life
- Observant: I comprehend it / I noticed that / Have you seen this yet?
- Insightful: I have a sixth sense about these things / I know that I know / I see the real story
- Curious: I wonder if there's more to the story / There's more to it than this / What else could we do?

Witty – Finding new ways to be clever and original
- Smart: I know what it's about / I get it / I know this
- Practical: Let's look at this realistically / Let's get to the point / Why not look at the facts?
- Clever: There's a smarter way to look at this / I think about it differently / They never saw it coming

EVALUATION FORM

1. The Flag Page session helped me to understand myself and how I succeed.

Strongly Disagree ☐ Disagree ☐ Neutral ☐ Agree ☐ Strongly Agree ☐

2. The Flag Page session helped me to understand others and how they succeed.

Strongly Disagree ☐ Disagree ☐ Neutral ☐ Agree ☐ Strongly Agree ☐

3. I am hopeful that this will improve communication with our team.

Strongly Disagree ☐ Disagree ☐ Neutral ☐ Agree ☐ Strongly Agree ☐

4. The Flag Page session was a valuable use of my time.

Strongly Disagree ☐ Disagree ☐ Neutral ☐ Agree ☐ Strongly Agree ☐

Comments:

_____

_____

_____

_____

_____

_____

FLAG PAGE® SOLUTIONS

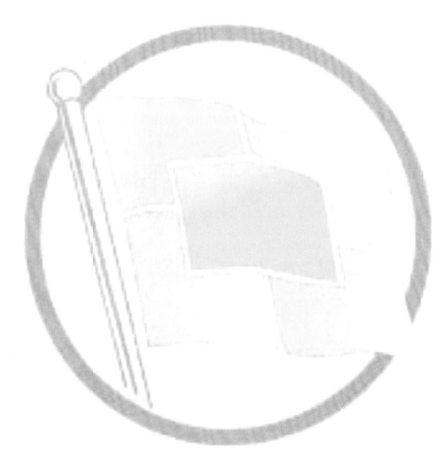

Laugh Your Way America
3475 Humboldt Road | Green Bay, WI 54311

866.52.LAUGH

flagpage.com
laughyourway.com

FLAGPAGE.COM

FLAG PAGE® SOLUTIONS

Notes:

_____

_____

_____

_____

_____

_____

_____

_____

_____

_____

_____

_____

_____

_____

_____

_____

_____

_____

_____

_____

_____

_____